2, 99

PIRATE MUSIC

Miriam Gamble was born in Brussels in 1980 and grew up in Belfast. She studied at Oxford and at Queen's University Belfast, where she completed a PhD in contemporary British and Irish poetry. She won an Eric Gregory Award in 2007, and the Ireland Chair of Poetry Bursary Award in 2010.

Her pamphlet, *This Man's Town*, was published by tall-lighthouse in 2007. Her first book-length collection, *The Squirrels Are Dead*, was published by Bloodaxe Books in 2010 and won her a Somerset Maugham Award in 2011. Her second collection, *Pirate Music*, appeared from Bloodaxe in 2014. She lectures in creative writing at Edinburgh University.

MIRIAM GAMBLE

PIRATE MUSIC

BLOODAXE BOOKS

ISBN: 978 1 78037 113 9

First published 2014 by
Bloodaxe Books Ltd,
Eastburn,
South Park,
Hexham,
Northumberland NE46 1BS.

www.bloodaxebooks.com
For further information about Bloodaxe titles
please visit our website or write to
the above address for a catalogue.

Supported using public funding by
**ARTS COUNCIL
ENGLAND**

Cover design: Neil Astley & Pamela Robertson-Pearce.

Printed in Great Britain by Bell & Bain Limited, Glasgow, Scotland, on
acid-free paper sourced from mills with FSC chain of custody certification.

For my parents

When autumn is over and the leaves have fallen from the trees with only the dark evergreens retaining their bulk which is at once a shelter and an obstacle to the passage of light, we see that we have never been alone in the forest.

JANET FRAME

ACKNOWLEDGEMENTS

Acknowledgements are due to the editors of the following journals, websites and anthologies, where some of these poems, or versions of these poems, first appeared: *Bear Review, BODY Literature, Causeway / Cabhsair, Connotation Press, The Dark Horse, Dear World & Everyone In It* (Bloodaxe Books, 2013), *Eborakon, Edinburgh Review, Éire/Ireland: An Interdisciplinary Journal of Irish Studies, The Honest Ulsterman, Irish Pages, The Irish Review, The Lifeboat, Neu Reekie!, Pleiades, Poetry Ireland Review, Poetry Proper, The Rialto, Shine On: Irish Writers for Shine* (Dedalus Press, 2011), *The Scotsman, Southword,* and *The Yellow Nib.*

A big thank you to Adrian Grima for allowing me to publish my translation of his poem, 'Andrew Dreams of Catherine Wheels'. 'Blue Nude' was written as part of a collaborative project with the artist Douglas Hutton and displayed alongside his work at Enniskillen Castle Galleries. 'Night' was commissioned by Katherine Lockton for a project celebrating the war poetry of Giuseppe Ungaretti and written in response to Ungaretti's poem 'Half asleep' ('In dormaveglia').

I'm extremely grateful to the Society of Authors for a Somerset Maugham Award in 2011; to Michael Longley who, as Ireland Chair of Poetry, gave me a bursary which enabled me to spend time at the Tyrone Guthrie Centre at Annaghmakerrig; to the Australian Centre at the University of Melbourne for awarding me the Vincent Buckley Poetry Prize in 2012; and to Jim Carruth for appointing me as the mentor on Clydebuilt 6. Thanks to the staff at Annaghmakerrig for always making me feel welcome, and to everyone who helped to make my time in Melbourne special.

For advice, encouragement and just general good companionship, I would also like to thank Paul Batchelor, Fran Brearton, Elizabeth Campbell, Ailbhe Darcy, Leontia Flynn, Peter Mackay, Paul Maddern, Eoghan Walls and Alex Wylie.

CONTENTS

Always Autumn

It is the season of the death of bumbles.
All buzzy resistless things
slam shut into windows
or self-exterminate in lights.

The season of the endless nights,
of TV poultices –
he who dances, he who sings.
The death of miniatures with wings,
muddled, and mid-flight.

Darwinian

If we had been shoebills
neither of us would have survived:
a second son and second daughter
from whom, after the dream days
of pragmatic action,
insurance against the first's demise,
our folks would have stridden, spurning
the hapless bodies,
carrying the fish and water
to the one who had cast us out
of the nest. No matter
that our folks lived right beside a river
or that the elder child confessed,
quite flagrant, to the filial atrocities
it dished out when they turned their backs.
But we should have been harder, louder!
There's the first child stuffing its face
on fish, the second scorned
for a puling baby,
left among the rushes to die.
The mother flicks an opalescent eye.

Alturas

The word spreads around the camp
and the men are summoned from the gold mines.
Dead silence. The Inca girls tell
string over their knuckles,
the healer heads towards the Temple of the Sun.

One by one, the white women birth
bleeding monstrosities:
some are tinier than kittens,
all gasp unsuccessfully for breath
like creatures spat against a rocky shoreline.

No one talks, or makes a sign,
although the Spanish shift to manage Quechua,
set free again the locked-up Inca prince.

Noon in Potosí. It is three generations
before one single woman has a baby that lives,
centuries until anyone works out why.

Normalisation

Pick a well-lit corner, and tie your animal there;
find the local radio station with the throwback music;
lose your coat, your woollens; secure,
if applicable, your hair. Now you are ready.
Take from the kit a metal curry-comb
and begin tackling the most intransigent layers.
Be economical but thorough: do not stint;
use strokes that are generous, semi-circular.
And so on with the dandy, the body, the duster;
bring scissors for the tail and under-chin,
bring mane-and-tail detangler. Bring
hoof oil for the feet and hair oil for the hair.
Work both of your arms together,
feeling your own skin get coated in the muck,
the dust and glair you have loosened from the animal.
Bring plaiting bands and even quarter markers.
Bring baby wipes and, for white feet,
for snips and blazes, baby powder;
bring hydro-glycerine to clean the saddle and the bridle.
Spend as long as it takes, and if
at the end of it you still do not feel satisfied
walk up the yard and ask them for another.
Repeat, until you know your left foot from your right.

Hotel Rooms

It's their simplicity we love –
their tendency to clean up
after themselves,
but also the limits on our baggage:
what will fit on five hangers and a couple of shelves;
our sudden transformation into this.

Like loving was a first kiss,
the calm-limbed body minus its head,
we put our things in order
(eyes avoiding the wall art)
and shove the emptied bag under the bed.

If only there were more channels,
and less of a clinical whiff to the air,
and maybe real milk,
we're certain we could make a start.

Instead, a telephone call
and if there's a dilemma, all the better.
We know that. We can play that part.

Bower Bird

All year
he gathers in
the mesmerising curios,
arranges – here –
no – here –
and rearranges
to his taste,
in its base
most eminently solid –
writ clear
in colour texture odour –
that flower, this
fragrantest of dungs –
though it's subject in
the ordering
to x-fold variations –

permutations, combinations,
Dear!
it's not quite, no it's not
quite perfect yet –
had he fingernails
he would scratch his head
feathers quite away –

and then there are always more –
more things, more
glittering phenomena
to be appended to his stack –
to the well-gauged
light and shadow of
his amour-shack –
this womanwork is never done –

they file by,
they doom to
ensnare him by
the ear
the eye
the nostril,
and before
he's aware of what
is happening
the place is
a sorry mess –

he begins the job
again;
he will sprain
what intellect's
amassed in
his tiny skull
toying with the heavenly
and unanswerable question
of
what a feathered female wants,
what may be guaranteed to bag one –

and she comes
and it is not quite
what she had envisaged,
personally, in her heart
of hearts –
down the leaf-strewn path there is
a better one –
the flower was
a fatal error –
and suddenly, so
suddenly,
his work is done;

he sleeps the vacant sleep
of eunuchs;
sweet bird
fear
the heat of the sun
or do not fear the heat
of the sun –

Personification

On the ferry to Larne, someone shouts 'That cunt of a curtain!'
and you're back where inanimate objects have malicious intent;
where soft furnishings are mischievous,
looking for trouble, and white goods present a staunch, rebellious mien
when, in levering them into the perfect slot, your da...encounters problems.

In the soft-pile carpet is the spirit of an elf
who wants to be out in the woods changing workmen to donkey kings;
the stereo, if it could, would seize, or sign itself away for scrap.
As for the old cloth deckchairs, summer nights to the tune of the midge
they rustle their foliage, flex their ancient wooden jaws like traps.

The Mare Spikes a Glassy Loch

      THE MARE
spikes a glassy
loch –
Foot,
FOOT, FOOT! –
and then
she crashes
headlong
into it

hot-blooded and
entirely live,
the crack of thunder
in her ears

Hoo!

with knees
high-stepping,
long-
lashed eyes
ablink,
the mare
spikes a glassy
loch

her mind
conceives forever

      BUT SKIES PASS,
the hoof-browned waters
clear

and the mare sets
foot, foot
foot, foot
against
this crumpled mirror –

Not
on your nelly, sir! –

and is gone like a bullet
across the moor,
sweat rivering her pelt

The mare, the chill loch waters

Reflexology

The plug on the hoover is greasy
after the flooding from the upstairs flat;
you think briefly
as you insert it into the wall,
then flick the switch and start to clean.

You wonder afterwards at your choice
which must have been one,
though you don't remember making it.
There is not even a terrorist,
this time, for you to say you won't be cowed

though you blame it anyway on where you're from: you say
into your own salty palm
that you learned to live like this.
Even your palm knows the argument is crude.
Its little patch of eczema stares you down.

Wipe

(for Mary Clerkin)

As my past is erased from the internet
pending the onset of professional life
(necking pints, it turns out, isn't a good look)
you are slowly losing your mind,
cursing, and cursing again your midway tack
between tradition and innovation, the lack
of memory stick and bookings book
that's brought you to this unforeseeable pass:
a Wild West showdown with a taciturn computer
that doesn't believe in anything, and has no history,
and laughs and laughs and laughs and laughs.

Films about Ghosts

(for Sophie)

The tape your mother made me in the summer of '99
when we, without having considered the practicalities,
would turn with two tongues out of the same head
phrases like: 'If you've never stared off into the distance,
your life is a shame', and 'Round here, nobody knows
your name', etcetera, etcetera, with the studied implication

that 'round here' was a dump, has long since parted
from its reel and slumped into the habitual loops and tangles.
And now, suddenly, new dispensations, a new angle.
Are these the makings of nostalgia? Fuck, I don't know.
But predictable patterns hurt no less for being so. And I
am not coming home today, or, even, tomorrow. Sophie. Hello.

In the Fall

(after Alistair MacLeod)

Made to travel on her own
she will trash the box, utter a cold sweat.
For her, knowledge is merely hope,
her head over the door.

A swallow travels on her back
in the summer, scissoring your path
as you stride down off the hill.
Horse heeds the hand she trusts,
will follow anywhere.

Horse foaled before you had her,
knows what it is to child-bear,
though horses will drive their own young off,
after a time, mares as well as males.

The home of horse resides in you:
you love her more, even,
than you might love a child,
her own love being blinder.
You arked this flood together.
Horse must never be betrayed.

Dressing Fleas

*If we do not mass produce products, we vie with one another
in the difficult, exquisite and useless art of dressing fleas*

OCTAVIO PAZ

Mr and Mrs Flea are dressed up
and ready for the celebrations.
He sports a neatly tailored waistcoat,
she silver-bordered asymmetric skirts.

They are the talk and toast of the party.

Sad to say, however,
a budding fashionista in the audience
catches sight of their duds,
and next year on the catwalks of Milan and London
the look is brazenly passed off
as the signature of the couture line
at the brand new *House of Insect*,
which in due course signs a cracking deal
with a high street shop.

I don't need to say the Fleas never see a penny,
and neither does their tailor,
who, five months out of the punishing year,
wrecks his eyes
and racks sleep-heavy brains
in the decking out of his favourite customers.

Though for him it was never about the money –
the fleas, dearest, could hardly pay,
and the tailor is in any case not a tailor
but a farmer from the provinces

going about satisfaction in his own, yes,

       his own unfathomable way
where the sun drops, faithless, to the littoral,
dead dark balling its fists against the light.

See him there, readied at the chipboard table.
He takes a swig of liquor.
See, dearest, how the inconsistent stars glitter and claw.

Mi Territorio

(after Pablo Neruda)

Here is my country. If you're wise,
you will turn on your heel and send it away.
Keep your bobbing sea lanes well policed,
your borders; once in, it will cling to you abjectly.

It's not valuable, even in its own eyes,
though its gorge rises at the slightest hint of a calumny.
In its vaults are discovered no recumbent stour-blown riches;
its mint gags on original currency.

Smooth turtle with a rubbled underside,
it can't get its head round concepts of money
and puffs like a filthy old factory stack its weal to ruin.
It is always changing its hue in company.

Here is the plumb-deep, ankle-deep midden of my country.
Do I jest, or speak the truth? And what of these analogies?

Blue Nude

Her lover is an island, far away.
He writes of breasts
tipped with raspberry fruit,
of arms like alabaster,
sends fat parcels
to the poetry press.
To her, he writes that
he's on the brink of greatness.
He's certain of it.
He just needs a little more time.

He sends her flowers,
and items of glass
to remind her of the beautiful fragility
(also because they're cheap).
The bed in the corner,
which you cannot see,
still smells of his papery skin,
his sex. It's the full guns sex
of the pauper and the abstinent.
The apples are from her mother.
He just needs a little more time.

And so she stares – petulant brat,
or woman with an eye too full to bear? –
at the deep blue vacuum
of the sea, the future.
This is just my narrative;
yours may differ.
For nudes are nothing –
form, structure, vessels for the roving self –
unless they match our stare.
And she – she declines it.
Either that, or she does what she's told.

Meditations on a Dead Pigeon

Take it away.
They will say that it was my
cat that killed it,
but I cannot accept responsibility.
Call in the men on their snorting, steaming chargers,
dredge up for me the plumy–helmeted ones.

Let them stride
and puff themselves out with unacceptable opinions.
Let them mouth shrill attitudes on women and the vote.
I will scrub, bleach,
pledge to don the bustle and the corset.
But please get it out of here – this clutch in the throat,

this drenched, foul fragment of the universe's
nether spaces, wings puckering round some intangible quote,
its eye the gelatinous pit of the albatross...
O ye lords steel-
shanked and sanctimonious, pray, take this from me.
Bring in, after all, the big boys. I can learn to live by rote.

An Emblem Thereof

Like Neanderthal man in his cairn
I have found myself here, face to the wall,
curled underneath the bounty of a duvet
which, though reeking of sex,
has been dubbed both a burial shroud and a caul.

How they weep, and tear at their hair!
How I hold fire, obstinately foetal.
They try the gods, but their prayers sway
weakly on the wind – they know this is no hex –
retreat into their mouths again, irresolute and fatal.

And sure enough, the word comes down
and in doing so confirms their worst suspicions:
Sorry folks; the next move is her own...

A civil war starts over who invented manumission.
It lasts x years, during which time I stay
in the duvet, scan Proust, cultivate the wax in my ears.

The Locked Room Mystery

(for Eoghan Walls)

Let's admit that it's come to a natural end.
The Golden Age is over;
new additions, however seeming miraculous,
can only in all truth repeat, repeat.

When, tell me, did our lives last depend
on someone getting the answer
(it didn't matter who): a poisoned dress,
a knife honed to a point so neat

the victim didn't register the wound?
Now, it's the field of the number cruncher:
out of imagination's wilderness
he comes forth bearing an ear of wheat,
a plot to which the average child could mime.

And yet we still seek the impossible crime.
Listen. There's a house, surrounded by virgin snow...

Cuba

Down nicked novabraids
connected to the skiff
we sink wide-lidded
into the element of love,
deaf, though not blind.
In this place speaking
is the work of signing.

Sometimes we sink too low,
almost brush the coral beds
with huge flat feet.
Other times, we rise
to the surface like balloons,
must dip slicked seal heads
so as not to break it.

It is too perfect to describe,
and I do not want to learn
the language. Let,
love, us have salt water
in our throats forever,
forget, almost, to breathe.
Let us not grow watertight.

Misrecognition

I am educating the computer.
So, I read it poems, information on whaling,
a centre-spread from the newspaper
about getting your feet massaged by fish.

I teach it finance, and international conflict,
endow it with the rules of football.
It says, 'I do not understand. Could you repeat?'

I indoctrinate it thoroughly
in punctuation, in possessives and plurals,
the troubled history of the Belfast mural.
I teach it fashion, and haute cuisine.

But oh, its radical innocence!
When it says, 'And that is twenty pines, please',
or 'The pound trees are wrecking the ecosystem',
I swear, Your Honour, it isn't coming from me.

Maighdean Mara

Give me your tongue, Scotland.
I'd meet you eye to eye
like a big eel gawping
in the gutter or the sink pipe,
startled, all covered in sand.

I would have you lift the grate
to me, Scotland, and reach
for my dumb, scrabbling hands,
plant me by your dirty dishes.
I would sing, and I would stand.

Précis

Cast on the beach,
       a momentary attraction;

erstwhile Goliath of the sea
       now the property

of the Lord Paramount of Constable,
       the rotting body his to sell;

which swell
       designates its fate not

the cooking pot but
       a series of pits,

the proud flesh there
       to await reaction,

the skull emptied of its fluid;
       It lights, beneficent,

towns with its bulbous head –
       lights the taverns, the assizes,

the conversations of the great and good
       while its massive carcass moulds;

is raised
       when skeletons

are à la mode,
       becomes a temporary hit

then a lone child's playground,
       apparatus, animal shit

Pirate Music

For ten plus years
they monitor the call,
deepening and desperate,
off range,
of a whale
believed to be
the only one
of its kind

no other marks
his particular rhythms;
with timbre
and timing out of sync
he is doomed
to understand
and not
to be understood

in waters
darker than
the devil's blood
he exists,
porous and piratical,
his temperament
which once was good
soured from
the endless lonely nights
and vacant days

(o fish
softly skinned,
o mammal)

where he sings,
adamant, tremolo,
of works not
shown to man

turn the dial;
he is in
your neighbourhood
and this is not
a parable

It

It comes in error up the estuary,
bleak remnant of the hands-off hand of God;

attains to overnight celebrity;
enters the bosom of a populace agog

with good intentions – *we want to make it
one of our own* –

and dies of racket
within sight of the English throne

where it is posthumously crowned.
It quite literally dies of sound –

of the rumpus of humanity
congregated in large numbers.

Later, interpreters of sonic bleep
intuit peace was not what it had come for.

Piero di Cosimo: *The Forest Fire*

Before chancing upon the fire, the artist
had spent a drear twelvemonth in the forest –
times, he'd later say, of the utmost despondency;
of dragging his forked easel day after day
like a schoolboy with a weighty satchel
to the coarse hide woven out of mud and wattles
where no creature of interest caught his eye.
He'd send, daily, his new man out to spy
with clear instructions as to what he wanted,
and every day, with his flat feet planted
like griddle irons upon the teeming earth,
the man (where do they *get* them?, he'd curse)
at every brown mole and scutty badger
would erect cupped hands and bellow *Master!*
A catch! in his well-trained, institutional voice.
Many a dark hour questioning his choice
the foiled great spent amongst the stinging nettles:
he dwelt much upon the running battles
he had fought with the *City & Artists' Guild*
(what had been their precise turn of expression?
Sir, your project is a digression
from the path of learning: we cannot spare
good students to you, for you waste their skills).
Then there was his chosen setting – what spoor
had led him to this sparse copse on the crown
of a hill that sat between two spurting towns
where soot belched arrogant from the chimney breasts?
And what had drawn him on this fool's quest
in the first place – were the city right to shake him?
At times, he began to doubt his very vocation.
Then came the day of the fire. The student
had spent the morning cataloguing rodents –
Master! A vole. *Master!* A stoat. *Master!* –

so he'd sent him off into the blue azure,
a child's toy bow and arrow on his back
and strict orders for him *not to attack*
anything moving – 'Shoot it at the plane trees'.
The student went obediently,
bent-kneed and ridiculous in city garb,
his big head jutting forth in concentration
like a sweet apple on the stalk of the crab;
the artist stayed on listless at his station.
Master! A sparrow. *Master!* A fox – fleet,
but plumb perfect in his lineaments.
The voice wavering across a great expanse.
He must have nodded off. Sketches of plants –
half-finished and surreally tainted –
lay smouldering in his lap; the student,
sprawling a few lengths from him, had fainted,
the bow and arrow gleaming by his side.
The choked air was thick with animal cries:
above, snipe, gunning like bullets, went
twanging in confused volleys into the trees;
the other beasts were making for the valleys.
Everything was motion, instinct, terror.
The artist readied his materials,
shifted his weight. They came slowly at first,
setting one threat against the other
(clear danger in the cover of the dell
with what was bound to follow from exposure).
Boughs fell; irresolute, they held their ground.
A stump-headed lion bulled dully around,
looking for his clean-limbed lioness
(her neat ears, her snub nose, charm of wetness);
the artist watched her slope off to the side.
A sleuth of frog-legged bears scuttling by
(Frog? Or were they more like an echidna's?)
passed under the flight path of a bat-come-pigeon
which held the artist with mistrustful eyes.

And then, at last, the semi-humanised
(the birds he could never approach right –
their fine-boned strangeness, their dolorous flight.
He ended blacking them in with charcoal,
though that, reader, is one to have and hold,
that you take with you to the other life):
you can see it in their faces – the strife,
the shame. Look at the little saddleback.
How he walks unwilling from the burning track
and out into the harshness of the world.
Look at the sad, pretty doe, so woman-eyed.
The artist sat among the flames. He sighed.
He looked on, with his finished sketches furled
beside him, as the cretinous student paused,
released blank arrows at the rump of a bull.
He watched as the bull proffered an expert heel.
Then he started on the road into town
his keen nose hot on the scent of *reputation*.
The student, he wrote off as a lost cause.

Vigilante

There has been a series of break-ins.
In each, a mendacious work was stripped from a wall
in a house in a terrace in a cityscape
through which the artist, like some latter-day Hansel,
and lured by the parings of his rotten soul,
from avenue to close to street
was dragged, we gather, on this orgy of destruction.

A sorry affair! Though we cannot guess
at his mental state, we hope this basic reconstruction
may breathe, poriferum, the nature of his crimes.
Data is minimal, barring the fact
the raid happened several years ago
to judge by the limits of the paintwork
and the out-of-date currency in scrolls
that was left in a cubby of every house.

Are you affected? Are you a victim?
Why not check your hidey-hole?
This man is armed with pap, and dangerous.
Please note, however, that this is just an artist's impression
of an artist. His profile is unknown
as not one citizen recalls his name
or what the image was they used to own.

Home

In the kingdom of the sun-shower
the same landscape's never the same;
where wind roars like thunder
and everything is always changing colour,
rain happens overnight
and washes the face of the world;
the water runs in gullies and puddles,
sullied and clear,
and suddenly spring up frog places,
lush basking spaces that as suddenly disappear;
cannily disguised as leaves
are left thumbing by the fringe of the road,
the ex-wonders,
though the swans are as solid as ever,
breasting the current two by two,
cool denizens of the fiefdom of flux.

The World Is Laced with Smells

The world is laced with smells
and the dog follows them,
pissing on anything that isn't legible
or that screams 'enemy!' or 'intruder!'
His brain is packed, as conch shells whisper
of waves, with hints of what has gone before;
his bladder is a well's endless supply.
He follows the track in swerved lines
as Holmes, not Watson, follows the law.
As for what he smelt, or saw,
in the coiled, darkling criminal mind
of a pickup truck from Tipperary
I couldn't say, but it must have been bad,
for it sent him back the long way
to his spit-daubed nuzzle-rug by the fire;
to flames, and dreams of Moriarty.
And I strode on witless into the mire.

Webs

Like the manuscripts in Emily Dickinson's drawer,
these ghostly works of wittedness –
more, and yet more! –
the artist having slipped out of the room.

By mist, by occasional sun
brought to notice,
world crafted over world, world netting the gloom
in quiet citadels flush to the shore.

Ghosts

As lines are steered through language,
and feet tread rooms
though we cannot hear their bitter patter,
and we follow the tracks of tyres
through mist-thrown fields
to the rushes at the water's edge
which won't, to human eyes,
separate themselves from their reflections,
cross-hatching like the shades
that muster a single hue,
somebody is surely steering you,
riderless thoroughbred pinned
to open air above the wall,
on out into the lake's electric blue.

Dido's Lament

He lost words like another child loses a ball
under the garden fence, or like an animal gets lost
in the woods up back of the family home
into who can say what dirt, what darkness.
In one go they're no longer his,
carried off like a trophy to feed the young
of some sharp-toothed predator of the night.

And there is nothing on his tongue
for the too-short remainder of his too-short life;
he's a boy without a voice, a boy
with thoughts stapled to the back of his head.

Months on, she's listening to the radio
and through this broken aria, he speaks to her

words trapped in music, *recitatives* of the dead.

After Keith Douglas

Poetry is like a cat
who, after many months and weeks abroad,
so long gone you thought it was dead
or at least a deserter to the lives of others,
turns up singing its welcome,
the tail, a question mark, threading your legs,
and apparently convinced that it is yours;
though on closer inspection
it may not be the animal you lost
that you now find purring by the fireside,
buffing its face with silken paws
in the wake of a sumptuous little meal.

Andrew Dreams of Catherine Wheels

(translated from the Maltese of Adrian Grima)

The Catherine Wheels run riot,
crackling through the night
like a herd
of excitable colts,
the sky their playground,
the earth
depository
of nuts and bolts

Where Andrew
breasts the wind,
heart pounding
a sympathetic spectacle
of imaginary colour,
greens shading into pinks
and oranges to indigos.
He's a new-enamoured lover

of the wheel-man's silhouette
a-lick with fire;
his conductor's wand in hand,
he's a red-cheeked general
after the massacre,
an explorer sighting land…

Your son waits
for the heavens to flame again.
But they're packing the wheels away.
And Andrew dreams of Catherine Wheels
long into the following day.

Childhood

When I look down into it I see a child who came to grief
off the same horse seven times at the same fence
and a man shouting 'Do it again! Leaning farther back.
Yer not leaning far enough back' –
and the child rises, dusts herself and does it again,

leans back further, and still the ground is bought
because the man's word on how to handle a drop fence
on this horse is wrong. She doesn't know,
even if she did could not protest
for the man's word on all things equine is law

and anyway buying ground is a badge of honour
round here, can't call yourself a rider without it,
so I look down silently and don't tell her
that the horse jumps out, that she needs to lean forwards,
and she sits tight and tackles the fence again.

Jiggy's Yard

With dirt a centimetre thick under his nails,
he pops the blackhead on my lip;
he cuts old Stanley's toenails with garden shears.
The portaloo is never emptied
and soap (soap!) doesn't exist, except for Min across the road
whose ma is particular, whose ma can see her.

The rest of us are like pigs in shite,
far enough from home to be incognito,
and though the bus to Belfast is always full
I always get a seat to myself.

To stop horses eating their beds
he sprinkles them with Jeyes Fluid and creosote.
Like everything, he gets away with it.
These – pure minging – these are the best days of my life.

Macken's Van

Macken is fucking terrifying,
but the blue-white van houses delights
and is, anyway, the only place in walking distance.

Up towards Lyle's, then on up,
as though you were heading for the Carnacaville Road
or the road that had Boden's on it – not Station, the other one.

Macken has a pair of Alsatian dogs,
sad cats and a sadder wife;
their house is like a junk yard,
but the van stocks Meanies that he'll sell you for 2p a pack
because they're past their use-by date,
also Tip Tops that blue your tongue.

You'd not want to be there when night fell, like,
or to tell him you're a Protestant.
Don't tell him you're a Protestant.

But the Meanies and that are great.

Mugs

Your brother bought us mugs
with the Union Jack on them,
not knowing his way
in the world of signs and emblems,
though for dates, for weird facts
he's second to none.

It's dinning your head
on a stone to tell him, the same
as trying to espouse
that he's *not* addicted to Coca-Cola,
or that, because we're older,
it doesn't prove we're rich;

strict meanings adhere to things
and flake from others
without rhyme or reason,
a comprehensible frame: to him
a mug is a mug
and the Union Jack a flag,

though, to be fair to your brother,
they're a good size
and perfect for coffee,
and though they live
in the darkest bowels of the cabinet,
knowing, we use them anyway.

Albrecht Dürer: *Lansquenet and Death*, 1510

Death – *How do you do?* –
offers an hour glass to the mercenary.
The mercenary doesn't want one
– *Not today; not today, thanks all the same* –
but he's been caught off guard and has to hear him out.
Death speaks in an impenetrable dialect.
He raves of the past and future.
The mercenary suspects he's addled with drugs.

Where – aimlessly – did a guy like this
get hold of a thing like that, the mercenary wonders, though.
(A lovely piece: true vintage, if it's a day.)

And Death is speechless, his long jaw drags
as the damned soul fumbles in a jacket pocket.
Here – buy yourself a burger or something. Don't let me catch you
*   here again.*

The Animal Room

Kingdom: Animalia; Phylum: Chordata; Class: Mammalia; Order: Carnivora; Family: Canidae; Tribe: Vulpini. Latterly an inhabitant of cities, the fox failed quickly, like the *passenger pigeon*. Last known sighting: Glasgow, 2023. Entry into the 'red' list for species threatened with extinction, 2021. Ate *rats*, *rabbits*, and *chickens*. Hunted for centuries by *farmers*, the fox became a popular figure in the urban centres, where it gained shelter and could sometimes be tamed. Here is a photograph of one begging in a TESCO *car-park* (location un-named). This one's stealing food from a plate. See the cheeky glint in his eye? The shift from a culture of blame to a culture of acceptance came late; experts speculate that, had it changed sooner, they might have survived. Hit the button, and watch the fox's *tail* light up, revealing it to this housewife: she is afraid it is going to enter the house and savage her children. She's carrying a *mobile phone*. In myth, the fox was a trickster; also a familiar and a messenger to the gods. You have ten minutes to write a poem. The buzzer will let you know when it's time to move on.

Perfect

Perhaps something chased it onto the road,
you said. Perhaps something chased it.
It looked neither left nor right
at the machinery of the world;
it pressed on like a fundamentalist.

A ton of metal and the hot fur kissed.
In the headlamps
it arabesqued once and fell to the side.

An Encounter

I spied the kitten on the road
in the country outside Dundalk,
thought to take it home with me.
This my first reckoning with a feral cat.

It bit, spat, even mustered a fart
from the reaches of its armoury.
I loosed it in a nettle patch
and went upon my way, whereat
the hissing slowly dimmed and died.

And there, on the uncontroverted throne
of its scalding freedom,
the little fucker sat, alone,
a snicker tall and a hiccup wide,
one single snarling animated burr.

Sun drenched the ears with glory;
dew glittered on the risen back like pride.

The Brutality of Koala Song

Hairy little don
with the voice of a sex-starved maniac,
your foot hanging out of the gum,
when pressed, should deliver a note
of Augustan sweetness;

it ought to be that you digress,
with well-meaning absent-minded intent,
on subjects of a day
that is thoroughly outdated;
you ought to sport
spectacles and a powdered wig.

You balance your bum
on the meanest twig
and sleep all day –
a twig that shouldn't hold you,
your bulbous weight;
your curled ball is ridiculous
to the sight.

                    Who
tutored you in this rapist's language,
little clerk, little Dickensian notary,
this bass guttural
that rocks the forest canopy
and that keeps me awake all night?

Gorillas will deface each other.
But you –
you have snuff in your ears,
you chew your poppies.
You're a natural non-sequitur.

Honest the hand
that chose to paint you grey,
with just occasional daubs
of black and white.

Dressage

I who would not be tamed
have turned my mind to taming you.
The world is out to rub our edges off:
we must bend and submit, bend and submit.

I don the jacket and the boots,
send forth into a marked arena decorous with flowers
the crazy horse I bought in Newry
and we dance to the manager's choice of pastel tunes;

an elderly aristocrat in a parked car
dictates her opinion on our movements
to a thirteenth century scribe: tense
or not tense, accurate or crude.

Why am I learning? Why are you yielding?
I want to drive smack into a concrete wall
singing I am an Antichrist, I am an Anarchist
at the top of my unacceptable lungs.
I never wanted to be in it for the long haul.

Bodies

A horse must learn to carry its own weight
through the use of its quarters,
to take a contact on the mouth
that's light but present, like the watchful eye of the law
when one is a fundamentally law-abiding citizen.
Or like the mind-hand's realisation
that a song does not work by sound alone –
that you must listen to the words and write it off
if you do not like them. That you cannot have
'fuck this', 'fuck that' and 'I'm not an animal'
without 'she's a bloody disgrace';
that you cannot merely sing along to the good bits
but must learn to carry your weight
through your quarters, take a contact on the mouth
that's light but present, like the watchful eye of the law,
oh brother, like the watchful eye of the law.

In the Blue Solitudes

Your Horse

Doesn't look like much
under the burden of the gear –
the pack saddle and the panniers,
the fly fringe improvised
from the tip of its tail.

Is without back shoes
and stumbles through the streets
of the tilting town,
its cobbled and concrete laneways,
where sour women watch
with faces like cobs.

Is carrying your bread
and your body,
your soul and your money,
for five hours straight
up a mountain sheer
as a pail – so high,
on cresting it you're drunk
on a single beer.

Relieved of you,
and loosed into
the lurid mountain grass,
is hard-bodied, metaphysical.

Could trample you to death but won't.

Tarn

You see the point of putting your feet in,
even full immersing in the shallow sides;
for you, it's about the shock
of the glacial water, that sudden slap of being alive.

You love your body and you walk round naked in it,
like a king, any chance you get;
your nude skin makes you indescribably happy.

I want the facet of a black diamond at its centre,
to hang over the mountain's plug,
over the mouth of hell;
I want to swing like a ludicrous fly in sap.
I cannot think the edges of it matter.

But I too love your substance,
will dust it dry for you in the crystalline air.

Sarcophagus

In the middle of the night,
stashed into a niche
in the mountain's side,
I plied your body with my body.
A silver horse stood over us,
waiting for light.

Eventually the cattle bells
returned over the hill
and the animal
relaxed its watching. You
started breathing.
O your skin was leper white.

Night

He's rolling the ribs of a person underneath his foot
because they don't like his cat;
they won't stop arguing that the cat looks evil.

Then he's by the hospital bed
of a man who might be his father
or else a bitter doctor,
and who is trying to murder him
for the sin of attempting to keep him alive.
I *don't* want *to live* the man says silently.

Mother! he calls and his mother comes
but she's naked and helpless,
and younger than she ought to be.
She's stitching a spray of autumn leaves
in precious silks,
a red jug but the colours are wrong

and for some reason this is more than he can bear
and he calls time and pulls the cord of the dream.
In amongst the gradations of red were greens and silvers.

He shifts in the trench.

The Others

They bid you drop half of life from your fingers
much as in the dream you dropped the token he gave.
Knowing you'd dropped it, you walked away
then spent the rest of the dream trying to return.

No one would come with you
through the streets of Edinburgh Belfast Melbourne
to find the necklace. Some said that it would not be there,
others vouched they had seen it stolen and recast.

There'd been crisp leaves piled to the kerb
where you dropped it, and you knew the necklace was amongst them:
hidden from view but still accessible,
you felt its presence there, waiting to be retrieved.

Gold aping the husk of the nautilus, ever-accreting pearl
of symmetry. When you went back the necklace had been tarmacked
into the surface, it was trapped in the body of that thick black sea.

Found

Your daughter dreams you are buried on a beach
which the IRA later affirm is true.
A beach is named and the whole beach excavated
but they don't find you.
Your daughter dreams,
your daughter with the dark rims under her eyes dreams
you are buried on a beach.
She sees the lights on the opposite bay,
she hears the wind skirl in the dunes.
It is cold where you are, and your daughter
with the dark rims under her eyes dreams
her body frigid; in the chambers of her ears like tinnitus
the tide reiterates its tune.
Salt silts on her tongue,
she wakes to the cry of the curlew,
thick water smacking on rocks.
Your daughter dreams, your daughter dreams.
Your daughter dreams the soundless blue.

The Horses

It's winter, maybe, the horses balanced in their canvas rugs,
heads drooped, sieving at the land and the air.
The time of hard winds, of bitten edges.
A man moves along the rickety perimeter
of red brick and suburban white plastic,
along what would be the alley out back if where we were
were a town of immodest ambitions.

But only the time-wormed can be dramatic in this way,
and where we are is a place that's new and fragile,
an inland commuter town estranged from salt and blood.
No gusty seadog has paraded here
swinging a head of hair like thin grey ropes and hacking of
encounters with the devil. The trees are seedlings,
folk using the bathroom wash their hands,
the teeth are clean. Even the horses, if you look closely –
for now we are panning back to the perimeter,
to the scrubby fringes of habitation
where coke cans gather in the hedgerows,
carbon-dateable by their specific hues of pink –
even the horses have an ersatz quality, it seems,
a lightness. Wind ruffles their manes
like it ruffles the blades of daffodils,
the stripped fingers of a hoarding hawking drink.

The horses gather in a clump at the top of the field
and the man tracks the boundary with his bundle.
He chooses, and in the pre-dawn darkness
he disburdens himself of something monstrous,
then he slips off neatly out of things.
He pursues the rim of the field with its wire and brackets,
its thran, abetting foliage. He dons his own features
as the soles of his shoes encounter tar.

What have the cloth-clad creatures to tell, what news deliver?
Of a child's flesh melting into the watercourse,
an unusual flush of blooms, when comes the spring.
All winter, the horses shy oddly but they are not noticed,
no one being much attuned to the ways of horses.
The white frontispieces open and close,
the cars spindle out their ghostly exhausts.
The reedy trill of an FM radio sings
Good morning, good morning, we've danced
the whole night through. Good morning, good morning
to you, and in the modest town no one suspects
though the wind rattles the placard on the tree
which states *The Wages of Sin* in blunt red lettering.
And, somewhere, a figure is laughing, far, far out to sea
with a laughter that means us ill.

Separation Creek

When I right myself and walk out of the sea
and feel that stab in the wrist – pain
of a type I never knew could come from water,
from simply staying in the cold too long,

it is my mother's bones in me:
the duff knee that tips her up onto her face
over rough ground, in the middle of buying apples,
and on which they will not yet operate

even though she falls out of the sky
and lands like thunder.
She has fallen so many times
she could be the human race itself.

The water is a manifest,
barium meal or unrequested X-ray,
showing up in the ridges of my body
everything that has happened, that can't be changed:

the years of anorexia,
the years spent uxtering fat children onto ponies,
my hands a cup that held their weight,
that held their weight from the wanting of the world.

We speak of age, your desperate desire for childbirth,
and I, a liver in the moment always,
I say to you that you cannot see your fate.
But when I right myself and walk

out of the sea, mine is written.
It says: *The earth makes what it wants of us*
and *What you've done is who you'll be.*
It's late. Elizabeth, let's go home

to the house where koala song
invades the night,
and what we cannot name or see
swings light over the canopy of the gums –

perhaps, someone says, a sugar glider
whatever that may be, whatever that may be.

NOTES

Précis, Pirate Music and **It** (34-37)

These poems take their inspiration from episodes narrated in *Leviathan or The Whale* by Philip Hoare (Fourth Estate, 2009).

After Keith Douglas (47)

'Poetry is like a man, whom thinking you know all his movements and appearance you will presently come upon in such a posture that for a moment you can hardly believe it a position of the limbs you know' (Keith Douglas, 'On the Nature of Poetry').

Found (65)

In interview for the *Storyville* documentary *The Disappeared* (BBC One, Northern Ireland, 4 November 2013) about the people killed and secretly buried by the IRA, Jean McConville's daughter said that she had seen the location of her mother's shallow grave in a dream.